God's Perfect Timing

Rev J Martin

ISBN-10: 1539592979
ISBN-13: 978-1539592976

DEDICATION

I dedicate this book to my family, for their constant love
and support.

CONTENTS

ACKNOWLEDGMENTS

This book would not have been possible without the support and encouragement of my family, and the inspiration from my Heavenly Father.

A special thanks to my editor and all the people a Pixal Design Studios for the lovely design work, and Amazon for providing the digital tools by which I can get my message out into the world.

Finally, I would like to thank YOU, for buying my book, may it enlighten your life and bring you peace.

1 Introduction

In life, it can seem that God never seems to get the timing right. Sometimes, no matter how hard we pray, it can seem like a loved one may never turn their life around, like the pain will never go away, or you may never meet the right person. It can feel like your prayers are going unanswered.

What I have found is, God has a perfect time to deliver what we want, but it is rarely done on our timetable or in the way we expect. If what you ask for is in line with your divine destiny, then the moment you prayed for it, God established a time to bring the promise to pass. God has a perfect time for a loved one to turn their life around. There is a perfect time for the healing, the right relationship, and the breakthrough.

It could be next week, next year, or three years from now. When you understand that the time has already been set, it takes off all the pressure. There is no need to worry, wondering when it is going to happen. You can relax, knowing the promise is on its way.

Matthew 21:22

If you believe, you will receive whatever you ask for in prayer.

When we pray for something and don't see instant results, it's easy to get discouraged, but if God gave you a glimpse of your future at the end of your prayer, it would change everything.

If 5 years from now, you were sitting in a new office, not only did you get the promotion, but head of your department. Your brother had not only turn his life around, but was running a successful business. Not only were you not single, but in your dream relationship.

With this glimpse, you would no longer be stressed; you would be excited. You would love going to work, stop worrying about your brother, and start living a healthy lifestyle, preparing to meet the person of your dreams.

This is where it takes faith; God promises the answers are on their way, but doesn't tell us when they will be. One of your perfect times could be next week; you get a phone call from your brother, saying he got the job that turns out to be the turning point in his life. Another perfect time could be on your birthday two years from now, when you get a break that takes your life to a new level.

The question is, do you trust God enough to believe He will deliver what you asked? Are you willing to wait with a good attitude, knowing what you need is on the way, or will you get discouraged, doubting, questioning him? Thinking you're destined to live the life you fear.

From today, you need to have a new perspective. God has a perfect time to turn your life around. No amount of worrying or sleepless nights will change that time. Don't let the negative thoughts make you think otherwise.

There is a perfect time for healing, a perfect time for the doctor's report to come back all clear. Now, stop worrying about it, letting it stress you out, asking questions like, but what if things don't work out, what if the pain gets worse, what if it's not my destiny to get promoted. If you ask these questions, you doubt that God is in control.

1 John 5:15

And if we know that he hears us--whatever we ask--we know that we have what we asked of him.

2 Getting On the Right Path

One of my favorite scriptures, and one I return to time and time again is Ecclesiastes. In its entirety, it is powerful, but the part I would like to focus on today is Ecclesiastes 3, verses 1-8.

Ecclesiastes 3 1-8

There is a time for everything,
and a season for every activity under the heavens:
a time to be born and a time to die,
a time to plant and a time to uproot,
a time to kill and a time to heal,
a time to tear down and a time to build,
a time to weep and a time to laugh,
a time to mourn and a time to dance,
a time to scatter stones and a time to gather them,
a time to embrace and a time to refrain from embracing,
a time to search and a time to give up,

a time to keep and a time to throw away,
a time to tear and a time to mend,
a time to be silent and a time to speak,
a time to love and a time to hate,
a time for war and a time for peace.

Whatever you may be going through at this moment, good or bad, will pass. We want the good times to last forever and think the bad times will never end. This selection of verses states there is a time for everything.

If you are going through tough times at this present moment, have comfort, knowing it will pass. If you feel like your world is tearing down around you, God will give you the strength to rebuild.

You may be deep in mourning, although the time of mourning has passed. God will give you the heart to dance to the legacy the person left behind.

There are perfect times in your future. You will come into times of grace, when all the worry fades away, when your relationship gets back on track, when good fortune puts you years ahead.

Habakkuk 2:3
If it seems slow in coming, wait patiently, for it will surely take place. It will not be delayed.

As it says in scripture, it may seem slow in coming, but wait patiently, for it will surely come. It didn't say maybe, or sometimes. No. It will be fulfilled; God has already set the perfect time for its delivery.

Sometimes, it can feel like you have asked so often that you just want to give up. Don't be discouraged. Do not be concerned about those that seem to get ahead of you. Enjoy your personal journey.

Doing your best is all that you can do. Be strong in faith, treating others like you would treat yourself, and God will deliver everything in line with your divine destiny.

Even after the worst storm, there is growth and tranquility.

3 Holding A Flush

There was a young man, called Philip, who believed he would succeed. He had tried many ventures, but nothing ever seemed to work out. He was advised by his friends to stop dreaming. They had given up on their dreams and wanted him to do the same.

This young man kept his cards close to his chest, but behind the scenes, he spent countless hours reading, studying, and working. He built a small home gym, started to run, and attended a public speaking club. His passion was always to inspire, although the method he would use to do so was never clear to him.

I chatted with him often. He was always very frustrated and confused why all his hard work never seemed to pay off. I told him what I am telling you; don't be discouraged, your set time is coming, God deliver's at the perfect time.

In early spring, he attended a health seminar. On the Thursday evening, as he was checking into his hotel, he met the person leading the event.

They started chatting, and the event leader was very taken back by Philip's understanding on the mind-body connection in the healing process, so much so he asked him for the titles of the books he read to gain his knowledge, as Philip came from a more spiritual viewpoint.

Philip discussed how he had always had a passion for health and hoped, one day, to be a speaker at a similar event, so he could inspire others with his knowledge.

On the last day of the seminar, one of the last speakers was going to be late as they got a flat tire on the motorway, and the event leader asked Philip if he would he speak for 20 minutes to fill the gap.

Philip agreed and delivered an excellent talk. He was also asked to be part of the Q&A at the end. The event leader was so impressed that he asked him to be part of the last few seminars being held in Ireland.

That weekend was Philip's perfect time to begin his journey as a professional speaker. If the guest speaker's flat tire happened two hours earlier, if he had not had a conversation with the event leader, if he had not had the knowledge and public speaking experience, he simply would not have got the opportunity.

A lot of events had to coincide on that weekend for everything to fall into place. What you can learn from this is, you can trust God's timing. Whatever you are praying for, asking for, will not be one second late. What set Philip apart from all his friends was, he never doubted God would deliver him success.

Instead, he prepared for its arrival, reading, studying, and working on his goals. Others tried to put doubt in his mind, telling him that his time had passed, but he never doubted that God would deliver.

If what you ask in prayer has not been answered yet, don't be discouraged or think God is not listening, which can lead to stress, worry, and doubt. Instead, do like Philip and prepare for its arrival.

Enter into a knowing; wait patiently, for it will surely take place. You are being directed daily by your Heavenly Father; learn to trust that whatever you asked for will be delivered at the perfect time.

There will be no need to go around doubting or wondering if something will happen, asking God when He will turn my child's life around, when He will heal me from my sickness.

When you live with the knowing that your child's life will turn around at a perfect time, you will recover from your sickness at the perfect time, with that knowing comes peace. It will take faith and patience, but that is the small price that God asks for giving you what you desire.

2 Peter 3:8

But do not forget this one thing, dear friends: With the Lord a day is like a thousand years, and a thousand years are like a day.

4 Childhood Prayer

When I was growing up, I remember saying a series of prayer, whenever I would be in the car with my mother. The one that stayed with me throughout the years is the serenity prayer.

Serenity Prayer

God, grant me the serenity to,
accept the things I cannot change,
Courage to change the things I can,
And wisdom to know the difference.

You cannot change the set time that God will deliver what you ask of him, but with courage, you can change from living in fear to living in faith. It takes wisdom to know you cannot modify God's timing, but you can change how you wait. It's necessary to have strong faith, to ask for something, and believe it will be delivered, never to worry, and never to doubt.

Only God knows what's ahead; sometimes, what we are praying for is not in line with what God has planned for us. It's important to learn to trust him. Sometimes, when we want something, and it doesn't work out, we can become disheartened, but then two years up the road, it worked out for the best.

Often, we can pray for the right things, but it's not the correct time. If it hasn't happened yet, instead of being frustrated or worried, asking, God, when am I going to get the new job I so desperately need? When am I ever going to meet the right person? When am I ever going to overcome my sickness?

When you feel like this, it's important to change your outlook. Have the faith to say, God, you know what is best for me; you can see the big picture. I will not be impatient or worry. I trust your timing. I know you will deliver what I need at the perfect time.

Today, we live in a society that wants everything right now; we have 24-hour supermarkets, bars, and restaurants, even gyms. We don't want to wait. You have only to stand in a queue (Line for my US friends), and you will hear people complaining that it is taking too long.

Faith is the natural part; the relationship with my neighbor will get better; I believe my business will grow. I know there will be better days ahead. It's the waiting part that is difficult.

Psalms 27:14

Wait for the Lord; be strong and take heart and wait for the Lord.

It says twice in Psalms 27:14, wait for the Lord. We need to combine our faith with patience. I believe great things will happen in my future, and I trust God will deliver what I need at the perfect time.

Learn not to get discouraged if it doesn't happen immediately. Don't give up because it has taken a month or a year; learn to live with faith and patience, knowing that what you ask for is on its way.

5 The King's Race

There was a king who was growing old, and he had no son to succeed him. He announced to his people he would choose an heir to the throne from among the young men of the country by a competitive test, which would give all an equal chance.

On the appointed day, a large number of young men entered. An individual test was made, and some failed, while others passed. This process continued until all were rejected, but three.

Each went through test after test, but all seemed equally able to meet them, so the king announced through his heralds, a foot-race would decide the matter.

The course was marked off, the judges were at their places, and all was ready.

At the start line, a man came up to each of the contestants and said secretly to him, "The king is taking special note of you. Do not run at the primary signal, wait until the king gives you a unique signal."

The three took their places eager for the race. The primary signal went, one bounded forward quickly, then hesitated and stopped; then another sprang forward, upon which the first started forward again, and they ran for the finish line. The third stood looking anxiously at the king and the two runners, murmuring to himself, "I can make it yet. I can make it yet."

The king gazed at the runners and gave no heed to the one still standing. The waiting man thought himself forgotten and soon realized it would be impossible for him to win the race and admitted defeat.

The two runners ran on at top speed, reaching the finish together. After the contest, they were all brought before the king. To the first, he said, ""You were told not to run until I gave you the signal, why then did you run?"

"I forgot," said the man.

Of the second, he asked the same question. His reply was, "I thought it was a test, and seeing the other running, I also ran as I didn't want to lose."

To the third he said, "And why did you not run?"

"Because you did not give me the signal, sir," he answered.

"My son," said the king, "I knew that you could run, but I did not know that you could wait."

So the young man found that the test was not a test of doing, but of waiting.

Isaiah 40:31

But they who wait for the LORD shall renew their strength; they shall mount up with wings like eagles; they shall run and not be weary; they shall walk and not faint.

6 The Hardest Lesson

Sometimes, it can seem the answer will never come. Sometimes, it can seem the Lord has forgotten. Often, I have had to say to my heart, "Be patient and wait."

Patience is the hardest lesson that many of us ever have to learn, but learn it we must, to see our divine destiny fulfilled.

Many people want change, but don't want to go through the waiting process. Waiting is a part of life and one of God's greatest tools for developing us.

The problem is, do we wait in the right or wrong way? If we wait the wrong way, we will be miserable, but if we learn to wait God's way, we will wait patiently and enjoy the wait.

It takes practice, but as we let God help us in each situation, we develop patience, one of the most important virtues. As we develop patience, we can finally feel satisfied, knowing all will be delivered at the perfect time.

My relationship with God is so much different now than it was when I was young. It is not nearly as emotionally draining. Every change I've gone through has made me more mature, stable, and grounded. We learn to trust God by going through many experiences that require faith.

By seeing God's faithfulness over and over, we let go of trusting ourselves, and gradually, we place our trust in Him. If He did everything we asked for immediately, we would never grow and develop. Timing and trust work side by side.

Hebrews 6:15

And so after waiting patiently, Abraham received what was promised.

If something is not happening on your timetable, remind yourself that God knows what He is doing; He has your best interests at heart; there would not be a delay if there were not a reason behind it.

While you are waiting, it's vital not to try to work things out, asking yourself what else you can do. This just leads to frustration. Learn to turn it over to God, stop questioning why something hasn't happened. Have the faith that what you asked for will happen at the appointed time.

7 Are You Working Against God?

What I see people often doing, rather than waiting, is they force things to happen. They don't see the result they want, so they ask for stronger medication; rather than listen, they walk away from a loving relationship. They lack patience.

Then they will plead, God why did you not answer my prayers???

What they fail to realize is, God is asking questions of his own. Why did you not wait for the healing? Why did you not wait and listen, instead of walking away?

Dream Home

A good friend of mine recently got married and was on the lookout to purchase a house to start a family. Peter wanted a house in the country similar to the one he grew up in, a homely place set into a hillside surrounded by a small forest.

In the meantime, Peter rented an old house in the nearby town; months passed and nothing. We spoke, and he had become very impatient and doubtful, mentioning often, maybe it wasn't meant to be. I told him what I'm telling you. God delivers at the perfect time; don't go rushing into a deal you may regret.

Another year passed. One day, I met him at a local community event, and he told me he just bought a house in Rockwood, a new luxury housing development on the outskirts of the nearby town. It was a lovely setting and had nearby woodland. It marked a lot of his boxes, but lacked the secluded feel I knew his heart was set on.

He went on to tell me, that he just could wait no longer; the lease on his rented property was coming to an end, and he just made the plunge. As we got talking, a lot of what he said was correct. No property in the area he wanted had come on sale for over five years, and he was not willing to wait for another five. He seemed happy with his decision, so I was happy for him.

A few weeks later, unfortunately, an elderly widow passed away who lived a stone throw away from where he was born, his dream location. The property and surrounding land were sold and split evenly among her five children. My friend's impatience cost him his dream home.

There is no need to force things, like my friend, to let impatience get the better of you. You need only to keep honoring God with your life, stay in peace, and be patient. God can open doors at a moment's notice. God will bring amazing people across your path; He will bring healing, grace, and happiness.

Don't go around forcing things you think you need, when God wants to give you better than you expect.

Psalms 37:4

Take delight in the LORD, and he will give you the desires of your heart.

8 Black and White

There is a big difference between God giving you something, and you having to work to make it happen. When we force things and don't wait or listen for God, life is a constant struggle; our life never seems to spread its wings and get off the ground.

If you learn to live by God's timing, there will be a supernatural grace, and life will flow effortlessly. Yes, you will have trails, but you will feel an inner strength, peace, knowing that all will be ok.

Be patient and let God open the doors. You will have to knock, putting in the hard work along the way, but God is always home, and He will answer the door; don't insult him by kicking it down with worry, doubt, and impatience.

As it says in Psalms, if you can be patient and wait for God's timing, He will deliver the desires of your heart.

That's what happens when you wait for God's timing. You won't have to settle for a luxurious house; God will give you your dream home. He will give you what He promised.

Patience is hardest when things are not working out. All too often, we think that, when our backs are up against the wall, we must do things on our strength. This is when many people make decisions that make matters worse.

When you're feeling overwhelmed by a problem and thinking of taking matters into your own hands, sometimes, you have to make yourself step back from the situation.

When you try to make things happen your way, stressed, upset, and worried, then God will step back and let you do it on your own.

When you have the wisdom and courage to pass it over to him, say, God, I trust you; you already set the time to take me out of his problem or difficulty.

There is a perfect time for my success. There is a perfect time for the healing, the promotion, and the house of my dreams. I will be still and know that you are God; you created everything, so I trust you will create my future.

9 Psalm 102

In Psalms 102, a man is overwhelmed with trouble and prays to the Lord. He goes into great detail to list all his troubles, how he was distressed, needing speedy answers, how his health is broken, how his enemies taunted and cursed him.

For 11 verses he goes on about how sad his life is, then in verses 12-13 he says, But you, O LORD, are enthroned forever; you are remembered throughout all generations. You will arise and have pity on Zion; it is the time to favor her; the appointed time has come.

For me, Zion is the church, you and me. Amidst all his trouble, he knew there was a time of favor in his future.

Like any relationship, it works both ways; you need to do your part and rest, be patient, expect great things. Trust that God will deliver at the perfect time.

We all face significant challenges in life; things are not going as you would like; you are stressed, depressed, and worried about your future.

Sometimes, God can delay what you want on purpose to test your character, teach you a valuable lesson, or show you his power in a greater way.

If you are waiting longer than you expected, that doesn't mean God is not listening. God wants to show his strength, his healing, his goodness to those who stand in faith and patience.

There are perfect times in your future; don't trouble yourself with when they are going to happen. God can see the big picture; He knows what is best for you; dare to say, like David, my future in in your hands.

Things may not have happened in the past, but don't give up on what God has promised you. Live, knowing that God has it all figured out; relax and enjoy your life while you are waiting for the vows to reveal themselves.

God has favor on its way, the right people on their way with ideas, and opportunities to put you years ahead.

If you will learn to enter this rest, trusting that all will be delivered on God's timetable. You will find that happiness and abundance will effortlessly flow into your life.

ABOUT THE AUTHOR

I live on the northwest coast of Ireland. I use this medium to share my true voice. I wish to enlighten others and help them to see that God wants the very best for them. We often make it hard for him to enter our lives as we focus on the dark clouds rather than the silver lining.

In this growing digital frontier I just want to shed a little light out into the world to light up peoples lives in the hope that they to will help inspire others which will slowly but surely change the world, even in a small way.

My Other Books

The Power Of Letting Go
The Power Of Choice
The Power Of Words

Made in the USA
San Bernardino, CA
22 February 2018